Let's Be Honest, Sis

Other Title by Award-Winning Author Jeannita Bussle, ED.D.

Sorrow to Shero

Pain, Power, and Peace

The National Coalition Against Domestic Violence (NCADV) defines psychological abuse as trauma to the victim caused by verbal abuse, acts, threats of acts, or coercive tactics. In "Sorrow to Shero," Dr. Jeannita Bussle gives an honest look inside her experiences. When the unimaginable occurs, she shares how she was able to forgive and heal. Additionally, Dr. Bussle discusses the hard life lessons that she has learned as a result of tragedy. Although "Sorrow to Shero" shines a light on psychological abuse and the importance of mental health, it is also a vivid reminder that God always makes a way out of no way. This powerful memoir is a must-read for anyone in need of hope.

"Powerful, Riveting True story of Love, Pain, Hurt, Dedication, Mental Illness and God's Mercy and Grace!"

"Powerful memoir that will encourage your faith to trust God when tragedy strikes."

Let's Be Honest, Sis

Are we truly our sister's keeper?

By

JEANNITA BUSSLE, ED.D.

Foreword by

Nishani Grigsby, MA, LPC-S

Publisher: Shero Management, LLC

Author Photograph: Niesha Lanae' Graves
www.nlgphotography.net
Cover/Interior Design: Mystic Circle Books & Designs, LLC
www.anitadickason.com

ISBN: 978-0-9999068-3-5 (paperback)

Library of Congress Control Number: 2021920479

Dedication

This book is dedicated to my mother and teacher;

Toni Clark.

Thank you for always leading by example through

your words and actions.

I love you,

Nit

Table of Contents

Foreword

This is a special opportunity for me to support Dr. Bussle in her second publication. Our relationship began when we were co-workers. Many years later, we would find ourselves inseparable.

In widowhood, she and I connected in a way unimaginable.

Last December, when I lost my husband, I unfortunately found myself walking in her footsteps. She and another beloved friend knocked on my door the next day. They did not come with voyeurism but with genuine love and support. She leaned in like no other.

This experience would be the bridge between her first book, Sorrow to Shero, me and this second book. Her first book outlined my experience of living with a narcissist step-father.

It is unfortunate that all too many of us live with one or more family members who have untreated mental illness. We have to seek help.

My mother shared with me that my step-father once said, "At least I'm not hitting you," implying that emotional abuse is less harmful than physical abuse. It is not. If you could know the depth of my scars, you might dial 911 or rush my mom and me to the emergency room.

Those scars are still present for me, along with emotional damage that resulted from broken relationships I've had with other women.

This book outlines the root of emotional turmoil that can develop in our connections with women, whether they are formed in friendships and social circles, at work, or even within our families.

I've spent the past eleven months diving deep into my spirit, working to heal from the loss of my husband. It is ironic that in my initial time of need for family and friends, many were absent. I found myself separated from all my in-laws to include five sisters-in-law and a host of nieces. I note this only because it is wrapped in female relationships. My husband had been the only boy in his family.

I worked to identify which, if any of the elements in this book, were at the root: envy, bullying, shade-throwing, betrayal, or unhealthy competition. I feel sick when I imagine that any of those dynamics could have been present while we were all grieving. However, I can attest as that they were.

I plan to work through the reflection questions Dr. Bussle has included. I hope I'll be honest when I examine how I have been guilty in my relationships with other women in my life. Her timing is perfect as I approach my big 50. Perhaps, if I'd had a little more awareness about how women can sabotage each other, I would not be in my current situation.

In addition, I am excited to be working on repairing broken relationships. As a clinician, I have to continually work on my own mental health, but I believe that regardless of our careers, we should do this. My therapist challenges me to keep the people I need in my life, and that it is ok to let go of others.

That has been my saving grace. Perhaps it has even kept me alive during this time period.

With no ill feelings, I am able to wave goodbye to relationships with people who would do me harm. I now have space to breath and move as I need to. Roadblocks have been moved out of my way. I know I was the one keeping them in my path, as I thought I needed the relationship. The truth is that I am healthier without them.

As you read this book and possibly recall some of your own failed relationships with women, know that it may be OK that they are no longer sentient.

One of my most difficult losses was that of a best friend. She did not die or move, but I likened it to a divorce or death. I damaged the relationship beyond repair. When her children were young, I made a comment about her parenting techniques that was rooted in old cultural norms that I believed she should have followed at the time.

I was wrong. I was wrong in the way I believed she should discipline her kids, and I was wrong for saying so. I have since apologized. Doing that was not enough to restore the friendship to where it had been. We are cordial but will never have the connection we had. I betrayed her by not supporting her ideals and beliefs. I may have even bullied her by trying to force her to do what I thought was best.

This hard lesson taught me to be slower to speak in my relationships with women. It taught me to evaluate what is in my heart. In this season of my life, I am working harder to compliment, instead of criticize. I want to support my sisters' efforts to succeed instead of standby or disparage them as they fail. I want to be able to say, "I've got you, sis," and mean it. It's my hope that because of my character, they'll believe me.

By the time you finish this workbook, you, Dr. Bussle, and I will all be connected in the sincerest of sisterhood.

Yours in healthy relationships,

Nishani Grigsby, MA, LPC-S

Nishani Grigsby is currently a Student Support Counselor in the Dallas/Fort Worth Metroplex. She began her career as an advocate for MHMR of Tarrant County. Nishani has 16 years of counseling experience and 5 years of experience as a classroom teacher. She has a Bachelor of Science in Psychology from Prairie View A&M University and a Master of Arts in Professional Counseling from Texas Wesleyan University.

Acknowledgements

First and foremost, I give honor, praise, and thanks to my Lord and Savior Jesus Christ. It is because of Him that this dream happened for me. Thank you, Heavenly Father for being a provider, protector, and so much more.

My village, thank you all for your unwavering support and prayers. Each of you are midnight hour type of friends and family. I am blessed to be on this journey called life with each of you.

Nishani Grigsby, thank you for pouring your heart and soul into the foreword for this book. The transparency and honesty in your words are a true reflection of who you are at your core. I love you.

Anita Dickason, thank you for bringing this project to life. There is no one else I would trust to push me to reach my full creative potential.

Introduction

#protectblackwomen

This trending hashtag has dominated social media timelines for the past two years. As Malcolm X once said "The most disrespected person in America is the black woman. The most unprotected person in America is the black woman. The most neglected person in America is the black woman."

I agree with brother Malcolm. "Protect black women" sounds good coming from civil rights leaders, and it makes for a great T-shirt slogan, but I would be remiss if I didn't acknowledge the internal damage that we as black women cause one another. Are we truly our sister's keeper? While we often cannot control how others treat us, we must take full responsibility for how we women treat each other.

As I reflect on the success of my memoir, Sorrow to Shero: Pain, Power, and Peace, I am reminded of the village of women in my life. My friendships with these women have played an integral part in my healing process. They never questioned the validity of my story when I described the abuse I endured by my late husband. In sharp contrast, when I read about claims of abuse by black women at the hands of black men, it is often other black women who attempt to discredit the victim. Two high-profile examples include Jennifer Williams of Basketball Wives and rapper Megan Thee Stallion.

I have personally witnessed black women create friendships solely because they shared a common enemy. I have also seen black women dragged and ostracized by other black women in the workplace for no legitimate reason. What is most disheartening is when these bullies are asked why they have such disdain for the victim, their go-to line is almost always "She thinks she's all that" or "Something in my spirit." These kinds of responses are intellectually lazy. They require no original thought. In fact, these women are scapegoating and won't admit that there's a deeper issue.

Why do some of us have a crab-in-a-barrel mentality? Why is it that we don't mind other women doing well, as long as they don't surpass us in social or economic status? Why is it that we secretly compete with even our closest friends? Why is it that we size up a woman upon meeting her as if she's auditioning to be in our friend circle? Why is it that we throw subliminal shade at women on social media? Why is it that we make a point to publicly proclaim we don't "do" her? Why do we betray a woman we refer to as "sis"? Why do we talk behind each other's backs and effortlessly share each other's secrets? Why is it that when we engage in these behaviors and the targeted woman cuts us off, we pretend to be the victim?

I have so many questions!

In Sorrow to Shero I openly admit that I had struggles with low self-esteem. As a result, I have been guilty of some of these bad behaviors toward other women. At times I have felt envious of another woman and wondered "Why her and not me?" But I have been able to see the error of my ways. I was willing to acknowledge that I had a problem. As a 40-year-old woman, I'm proud that I no longer exhibit this behavior.

Feelings (which we consciously experience) are normal. Emotions (which we're either conscious of or are buried in our subconscious) are normal. What becomes problematic is when our internal struggles negatively impact the emotional state of someone else. Our insecurities are not an excuse for us as black women to treat each other the way we do. The emotional wounds that some of us have inflicted on each other are inexcusable. If black women are ever going to be protected, we must start by protecting one another. We cannot expect others to do for us what we are unwilling to do for ourselves.

"Envy is the art of counting the other fellow's blessings instead of your own."

~Harold Coffin

1

Envy

I will never forget the day a former associate told me that her childhood friend had an incurable sexually transmitted disease. I knew the friend whose privacy had just been violated: an attractive, educated, successful black woman with a beautiful family. I was fascinated by the ease with which this information flowed from the lips of this backstabber. Not only did she effortlessly share this beautiful woman's innermost personal secret, she exuded joy, which was evident in the smirk on her face. What bothered me the most was not the gossip I had just heard. I was more disturbed by the obvious satisfaction of this so-called friend. This situation was a reminder to never reveal details of my life that I do not want repeated.

What I would like to examine isn't gossip. We all know people who are messy at their core. These individuals cannot hold water. Messiness is for women with too much time on their hands. The best way to combat these individuals is to steer clear of them.

I am more interested in why some of us gain satisfaction from the downfall of others, even our so-called friends.

In *Sorrow to Shero* I detail my late husband's horrific death and the aftermath. One of the topics I discuss is gossip about my family and obsessive concern regarding my finances. Word travels fast, and I found out my life was being discussed by individuals that I barely knew or did not know.

I found it sickening that people could take comfort in knowing I could potentially lose everything. But this was also the piece that intrigued me. I am interested in examining the why.

Envy is defined as a feeling of discontentment or resentful longing aroused by someone else's possessions, qualities, or luck. Jealousy is often confused with envy, although the two words are used interchangeably. Jealousy tends to be focused on keeping what is ours. For example, if someone covets your new Jimmy Choo shoes, they may feel envious. If a woman flirts with your husband, you may feel jealous. Both can produce anxiety, depression, and compulsive worry.

For the purposes of this chapter, I will focus on envy.

Envy is a real emotion, however, our society tends to shame those who point it out, even when it's obvious. I have seen memes on social media that label women as delusional or narcissistic when they are pointing out alleged "haters." It would be naïve not to acknowledge that this is sometimes true: some women believe everyone is envious of them. They think more highly of themselves than they should, and they come across as self-absorbed.

However, envy is still real. And it can be destructive when it goes unchecked. Sometimes there is legitimacy when a woman is accused of being envious of another woman.

I believe the reason my former associate felt joy when disclosing such personal and embarrassing information about her friend was due to her having envied the woman. Her perception of suddenly having a one-up or "gotcha" revealed itself through her facial expression. This piece of information gave her a high.

I was disgusted by this information sharing and I never looked at the woman the same way after that. I knew that if she could betray such a close friend, I was also an easy target. No one was safe.

Envy is at the heart of why many female relationships do not last. It is the reason drama forms within so many friend circles. I am blessed to finally have friendships that are drama free and genuine, however, this was not always the case. Both from working as a school counselor and my personal experience, I know that envy can fester in girls and young women from a very young age, even in elementary school.

Middle school is where everything turns up. Some of the most vicious fights I've ever witnessed have been between 12-to-14-year-old girls. When students are in conflict, if the school counselor is made privy to the situation, they intervene.

There were times when I mediated a conflict between two young ladies, and the envy in one of them was crystal clear to me.

One particular instance stands out, which I never forgot. Two eighth grade girls were called into my office because of conflict. Student A was tall, tomboyish, decently dressed, attractive, and popular among the female students. Student B was a beautiful, curvy fashionista who was desired by all the eighth-grade boys. It had been reported that student A had been harassing student B. In my office, I asked student A why she did not like student B. She went silent. This young lady had absolutely no justification for her behavior, but to me it was obvious.

I made a few observations about these girls, and as we talked my feelings were validated. Student B seemed completely unbothered by student A. She spoke very little, but when she did interject, she read student A for complete filth. It came out that student A liked a boy who was smitten with student B.

What I observed in this interaction was that it didn't matter that both young ladies were attractive and smart. Student A was intimidated by student B. She was envious. She wanted what student B had: the affection of a certain boy. Student B did not have to do anything directly to student A, nor did she have to speak negatively about her. The offense was created in the mind of student A. Student B's mere existence bothered her.

This scenario is not isolated to middle-school girls; it can manifest through high school and beyond. I have noticed that the older some women get, the craftier they become in their attacks. When women refuse to admit why they have such disdain for another woman they make up a weak excuse. No one is willing to admit "I'm just a hater." Rather than state the obvious, labels requiring no intellectual thought are slapped on the target.

To quote a few:

"She thinks she's all that."

"She has a bad attitude."

"She's a bitch."

"She doesn't speak."

These statements are weak and corny. What is most disheartening is that even if they are baseless, started simply because a woman is envious, they can still make or break the person's reputation.

Unchecked envy can lead us down a dark path. It can cause us to betray those we should be learning from or making money with. Envy can cause people you've helped to turn against you. People are very quick to forget all the good things you do. Once they get what they want, you become disposable. Their deep-rooted envy manifests when they realize they cannot use you any longer. These types of individuals were only tolerating you to begin with; they never truly cared about you. Unfortunately, these sorts of fake friendships are far too common.

Envy in friendship can rear its ugly head in a variety of ways. One is when friends become envious of relationships among other friends in the same circle. Women tend to be territorial. Instead of treating each other like sisters, some of us treat each other like property. We may take the stance of "You are my friend!" or "I've known you the longest." This is when the childish battle for the best-friend award begins.

Some women feel threatened by their close friends' relationships with other women even if they know all the involved parties. I find it deeply disturbing, but this is a real issue with some adult women. This territorial mindset will cause a sister-friend to act like a scorned side-chick. The envious woman will tend to act out as a side-chick would, causing tension in the group. Then childishness such as posting subliminal messages on social media begins. Sometimes the scorned woman will even unfollow or unfriend the woman at the root of her envy. The woman will make up excuses for the fallout, even though she created it. She will come up with a lame excuse for why she has an issue because she is not mature enough to admit her internal conflicts.

Envy in friend circles can be emotionally dangerous. The targeted woman may become ostracized if the other women in the group are blind to what is occurring. Sides are taken and peoples' character is questioned. Rather than discuss the issue like rational, supportive women, silent treatment may be applied and continue for weeks, months, or even years.

Although friendships are ruined for a variety of reasons, in my personal and professional experience, envy lies in the ruins. It is often the true issue being disguised by a surface-level offense.

Let's be honest and admit that we feel a certain type of way when another woman gets the promotion we wanted. Maybe we didn't even want the promotion, but we're still bothered by her shine. Some of us get into our envy when a friend gets a new car or a bigger house. Some of us feel envious when a friend puts forth effort to lose weight and glows up in appearance. Rather than compliment her and ask her for her secrets to success, some of us make snide comments about the tight, revealing clothing, showing off her new figure.

For me, it's the envy. We've all experienced it, whether we've been perpetrators, recipients, or both. Instead of being in denial about this emotion, we should normalize acknowledging that it exists.

There is a fine line between being inspired by someone and being envious of them. We must be careful not to confuse the two. A person you inspire is encouraged by you to be better, do better, and achieve more. You may serve as a mentor of sorts. Women may look up to you and view you as a professional or personal guide. In contrast, an envious person may be inspired by you but still hate you.

As emotionally damaging as envy can be, it can also impact us physically. Envy can cause our bodies to feel stressed. This is not surprising, as research points to a direct correlation between mental and physical health. As a result of stress, the body can develop ailments such as insomnia, high blood pressure, and a weakened immune system. So, it is crucial to address this negative emotion because it can literally be a matter of life and death.

The first step in addressing envy is self-awareness. We must learn to acknowledge our feelings and be honest about them. Self-awareness helps us identify how our emotions affect our behavior. As women, when we feel ourselves developing negative emotions toward a sister, we should first look inward. Instead of trying to justify our disdain, we should do a heart check to determine the real issue. If we are honest with ourselves, some of us will come to realize that at times we are the source of the problem. Although looking at ourselves in the mirror can be hurtful, it is necessary.

If we can become aware of our emotions, we will have an easier time managing them. Effectively managing them can motivate us to achieve our goals. By focusing on our goals and aspirations, we may be less likely to envy our sisters for their achievements. Effectively managing our emotions can give us discipline in our actions. A woman who's aware of feeling envious can think before she speaks and pray before she acts. She can acknowledge her emotions rather than being in denial about them. She can do the internal work to heal negative and undeserving emotions toward her sister.

Reflection and Discussion Questions

1. Think of one or more women or girls whom you envied in the past or currently envy. Write down their name.

____

____

____

____

____

____

2. What was it about each of these people that made you feel envious?

____

____

____

____

____

____

____

3. Were any of these women (or girls) your friend? If so, did your internal struggle negatively impact the friendship?

4. Do you still have a connection to any of these people? If so, do you still struggle with related envy?

5. Is there anything you believe can help you move past your envious feelings? What are some ways you might be able to find peace with the person you've envied or still envy?

6. List several things you're thankful or grateful for in your life. How do you think thankfulness and gratefulness are related to envy?

____

____

____

____

____

____

____

____

____

____

____

____

____

Then Peter opened his mouth, and said, Of a truth I perceive that God is no respecter of persons.

Acts 10:34

"Throughout life people will make you feel mad, disrespect you and treat you bad. Let God deal with the things they do, cause hate in your heart will consume you too."

~ Will Smith

2

Bullying

The main types of bullying are physical, verbal, cyber, and social. All four can occur from the elementary-school years through adulthood.

In this chapter, I'll focus on social bullying, the most frequently exhibited form that I have observed among women. This type of bullying is often hard to recognize or prove.

Australia's National Centre Against Bullying (NCAB) states social bullying is designed to harm someone's social reputation and/or cause humiliation. NCAB includes lying, spreading rumors, mimicking, encouraging others to socially exclude someone, and damaging someone's social reputation or social acceptance as forms of social bullying.

Whether we like it or not, or choose to admit that this is true, these tactics exist. Some of us are perpetrators of bullying or know someone who is.

What gives me the most unrest is when the bully is revered in their community or social circle. These individuals are the most lethal because of their power and influence. If the targeted woman dares speak out against the revered figure, she is likely to be ostracized. There are times when tangible evidence exists, and some women still refuse to see the truth because they would rather follow whom or what is popular. A bully would rather run a smear campaign against her than to acknowledge the truth in her words. When we can no longer ignore facts that we've refused to see, the most basic excuse ever known is thrown: "I didn't like how you said it."

I find this excuse comical. This statement should be on the deflection wall of fame. The truth is that it doesn't matter how someone states a harsh reality if it is not what we want to hear. A person could sing something in an angelic voice from the choir stand and some people would still find a reason to have a problem with it.

Divide- and-conquer tactics have been used for centuries, such as by the British Empire. Successful leaders understand it is a powerful strategy for pacifying groups or individuals that resist control. When a group of people is united, they become difficult to overtake. Groups broken into smaller units are weaker and, therefore less likely to oppose the sovereign.

We can also see divide-and-conquer strategies used in social circles and communities. It is an evil strategy rooted in manipulation and narcissism. The obsessive need to be the "queen bee" causes some women to resort to these tactics. If the queen gets frustrated by her inability to control the target, she will attempt to control how others view the target.

These sorts of women are dangerous.

Their first step is to gain the victim's trust. The woman may allow the future bully into her home and personal life. As a result, the perpetrator slowly gains the trust and admiration of the victim's friends, colleagues, and even family members. This is done strategically in order to then be able to get the victim's support system to turn against her. When the target woman realizes what's happening and decides to confront the perpetrator, the bully pretends to be the victim. This woman may even pray for her victim in an effort to prove her innocence and genuine intent. She will go to any lengths to gain supporters by making herself appear to be spiritually and mentally mature, while she is actually a narcissistic wolf in sheep's clothing.

What is so disturbing about divide-and-conquer tactics in social situations is that they're often used by those we would least suspect. The target is usually blindsided. By the time she realizes what is occurring, she has been isolated from her support system.

There is hope for those who have fallen victim to bullies. God is our vindicator. He sees everything. Even if these women have power and influence, they are no match for the God we serve. Our heavenly father has a way of bringing the unjust to their knees in one way or another. Always remember that we reap what we sow. No one is exempt from spiritual law. Your race, gender, and socioeconomic status does not matter. God will eventually pull the covers back and reveal the truth. We never have to seek revenge because these perpetrators always destroy themselves. God will even turn around and bless you in front of them.

Social bullying can occur anywhere. It not only happens in social circles, it goes on in the workplace. Black women in particular have a hard time with it. It's bad enough that we have to go the extra mile just to be afforded a seat at the proverbial table. We have to go above and beyond to prove our worth and competence at work. I am deeply disturbed because sometimes it is black women who target and bully other black women in the workplace.

On my web show, I interviewed a close friend about the

relationships black women have with one another. One topic we discussed was the black woman in corporate America.

I was disgusted and angry when my friend described something she experienced with a black female supervisor. This supervisor felt threatened by the genius that is my friend. She was the total package: attractive, highly educated, and successful. The problem was that so was my friend.

Some black women want to be the only one in a certain space, the only chip on the cookie. They believe there's not enough space for everyone. When another equally fabulous black woman comes along they get intimidated.

Unfortunately, this supervisor was not alone in her behavior. What my friend described occurs far too often. There are women like this everywhere, from corporate America to the world of higher education, and even the church.

Women in the church can certainly be bullies. Let's admit that we can tell someone "God bless you" yet put stank on it. For years I was completely turned off by the church because of its blatant hypocrisy. For example, I felt that older women in the church should serve as role models for younger women. The Bible is clear about this: Titus 2:3 states that "Older women similarly are to be reverent in their behavior, not malicious gossips…" Although many women in the church do set positive examples for younger women, some do not.

Before I was married, I was a young, single woman in a black church. My parents were ushers, and although I wasn't very active in church activities, I knew many of the church members. I had women whom I could look to for mentorship and support. These women prayed for me through the darkness and celebrated my winning seasons.

Unfortunately, not all of my experiences with saved and sanctified women were positive. I remember the looks I received from a few married women if I stood too close to their husbands or even said hello. I remember thinking that these women were ignorant for their rude dispositions and I tried to figure out what I had done to irritate them. Was I flirtatious? Dressed inappropriately? Did I give off man-stealing vibes? The truth is that I'd done nothing wrong.

I challenge my married sisters to stop looking at every single woman as if she wants to snag your husband. I challenge you to work on your self-esteem. While some women are indeed scandalous and sleep with married men, that's not always the case. Your distrust of a certain single woman may be justified, but perhaps you should instead direct your concern at your husband. Yes, your husband could be the issue, sis. That single woman may not want your man; he may want her. He may lust for her, not the other way around. Never hate the player. So instead of treating the woman like a jezebel, try praying for her. Better yet, pray for your husband and the health of your marriage.

When poor behavior in church is pointed out, the line delivered from the pulpit is almost always "No church is perfect. The church is imperfect because we are here." Although this example is literally true, as parishioners, we have a social responsibility to make all people feel welcome in a place of worship.

I have witnessed some of the darkest forms of hypocrisy in the black church, from pimps in the pulpit to pedophiles on the praise team. The problem with negative experiences in church is that its purpose, saving souls through the teachings of Jesus Christ, gets lost in the drama.

Many people are already skeptical of the church and Christianity. When new people decide to show up for a service, it takes very little to turn them off. Christian women conducting themselves as mean girls in the sanctuary is certainly one reason. Unfortunately, some women who have had negative experiences in church never return, and thereby miss out accepting everlasting life through our Lord and Savior. It takes a certain level of maturity to recognize that a few bad apples do not have to spoil the entire bunch.

The mother-in-law (MIL) and daughter-in-law (DIL) relationship can be very complicated. I have witnessed healthy, positive versions of this relationship in which there was genuine love and respect from both women. However, in some situations, the dynamics can become toxic. With this complicated relationship, I believe bullying deserves the most attention because the other four behaviors (envy, shade throwing, betrayal, and competition) often lead straight to it.

I remember feeling envious of a MIL-DIL relationship that resembled my own with my former MIL. Although she and I were never super close, we had a decent relationship until the day my husband and I got married. That's when all hell began to break loose. Our in-law relationship went from love and respect to every negative emotion and behavior discussed in this book.

The Bible is very clear about the relationship between a child and a parent. Ephesians 6:1-3 states that "Children, obey your parents in the Lord: for this is right. Honour thy father and thy mother; that it may be well with thee, and thou mayest live long on earth." The Bible also says in Ephesians 6:4: "And, ye fathers, provoke not your children to wrath: but bring them up in the nurture and admonition of the Lord." Parents often overlook and sweep this particular scripture under the rug. The bottom line is that both child and parent are to show respect toward one another. This includes respecting the adult child's marriage.

Let's be honest and admit that there are circumstances in which a MIL is completely justified in disdain toward her DIL. As a mother to a son, I would be furious if my child brought home a woman whom I believed to be unsuitable as a wife. No mother wants a DIL who is boisterous, curses like a sailor, dresses like a whore, is disrespectful, or tries to physically fight your son. Although a mother's instinct is to protect her child, it's his job to choose his mate. According to Proverbs 22:6a, our role as a parent is to train our child in the way they should go. Proverbs 22:6b goes on: "And when he is old, he will not depart from it." Moms are their sons' best examples regarding what to look for in a wife. Sometimes our children will go astray despite our positive examples, but being a parent also means allowing your grown children to make their own mistakes. Of course, we are allowed to voice our opinions if and when we're asked. But afterward, our role is only to pray and wait.

On the other hand, we must be honest and admit that some MILs take issue with *any* woman their son chooses to be his wife. It doesn't matter if the wife is educated. It doesn't matter if the wife adores the MIL's son and treats him like a king. It doesn't matter if she is a working mom and contributing financially to the household. It doesn't matter how respectfully the DIL conducts herself. Nothing matters. The MIL will find any reason to dislike the DIL, regardless of how wonderful she may be.

I am fascinated by the mother-in-law who is herself a wife and still bullies her daughter-in-law. I've heard horror stories about MILs ostracizing their DILs, for instance by not letting them attend family events, turning the son's siblings against the DIL, and even being overtly disrespectful. I find it impressive that a married woman would have this much time on her hands to pry her nose in her adult son's marriage.

Some argue that hurt people hurt people, and that perhaps this type of MIL was bullied by her own MIL. I think that's a poor excuse. In fact, I think it's all the more reason for this type of MIL to try to embrace her DIL. I would think this woman would bend over backward to ensure that her DIL doesn't experience what she did. Being hurt does not give us the right to hurt others, nor is bullying some sort of rite-of-passage when joining a family.

Sometimes bullying by a MIL is done in the dark: she may smile in her DIL's face, but behind her back, speaks negatively about the woman to her son. Some may read this and argue that it is the son's responsibility to check his mother; to put her in her place. I absolutely agree, but this book is about relationships between women. Let's stick to the issue at hand, as if the mother-in-law were to mind her own business, there would be no need for the son to check her.

Secondly, some MILs may be envious of their DILs. Maybe the DIL reminds her of everything she never became. Maybe the MIL is miserable in her own marriage. Sometimes the MIL has never had a husband of her own, and she's always looked to her son to fulfill her emotional needs. Maybe the son has financially supported his mother, and she fears that monetary support will be cut off with the presence of the DIL. Sometimes the MIL simply cannot stand the fact that she is no longer her son's top priority.

As selfish as all of these attitudes may be, these women are only human. MILs come from all walks of life. They could be the friendly neighbor who waves as you drive by, or they could be your boss at work. These women may sit next to us in church, and might even serve on the deaconess board. You never know what someone is truly like behind closed doors.

The Bible states that a man is to leave his father and mother and cleave to his wife. If we claim to read the Bible, then we must read it in its entirety and check our hearts. Let's be honest and admit that we may have a mother who needs to be set straight. Some of you may be fully aware of your mother's horrible treatment of your brother's wife, for instance, yet you say nothing to her. Letting this slide is called being an enabler.

The aftermath of bullying can cause lifelong psychological damage. Maya Angelou once said, "People will forget what you said, people will forget what you did, but people will never forget how you made them feel." I agree with the latter part, however, I believe people *do* remember what you said, and they *also* remember what you did.

I remember words spoken to me as a child, whether they were loving or damaging. I must give my parents credit because they both made a point to always speak life in me.

Unfortunately, all adults do not take this stance with children.

As parents, we must also be careful about how we treat our children's friends, even the ones we do not care for. We may look at these children as bad influences on our sweet little angels, but the hard truth is that sometimes our own children are the issue. Let's be honest and admit that our child may be the one who's a bad influence. Your child is not always innocent, sis.

When I was growing up, a couple of my friends had parents who swore that I was a bad influence. They did not want their children to hang around me, even though they had absolutely no reason. Years later, these same children became scammers and thieves. I, never became a thief or a scammer, so these parents had to eat the words they'd spoken about me. They also had to realize that anyone can fall short of the glory of God, even their own children.

Parents, teachers, pastors, neighbors, bus drivers, lunch aides. All have the ability to scar a child. Children do remember. They remember what you said, what you did, and how you made them feel.

We must plant a seed of love in all children. We must speak life in them early to build their self-esteem. We must hope that they do not grow up with low self-esteem, lacking emotional maturity and subsequently metamorphosing into mentally unstable bullies.

Reflection and Discussion Questions

1. Think of a time when you were bullied. Describe your experience.

2. Does the memory of being bullied still affect you? If yes, in what ways?

3. Have you forgiven the person who bullied you? If so, what was your process for forgiving and healing? If not, what is keeping you from doing it?

4. Were you ever a bully? Describe the scenario.

5. If you were a bully, did you apologize to the victim? If yes, what was the end result? If no, why not?

6. Have you forgiven yourself for your bullying behavior? If so, how has this affected you since that time?

7. If not, do you believe it's possible for you to forgive yourself, move forward and improve in this area?

____

____

____

____

____

____

____

____

____

____

____

____

But to you who are listening I say: Love your enemies, do good to those who hate you, bless those who curse you, pray for those who mistreat you.

Luke 6: 27-28

I'd rather have an enemy who admits they hate me,

instead of a friend who secretly

puts me down.

~*Unknown*

3

Shade Throwing

We have all done it. Whether with close friends or with strangers in a check-out line, all of us have been guilty of what our society calls throwing shade. As a person with a sarcastic sense of humor, I admit that throwing light shade has been one of my strong suits. I believe shade throwing can be fun among friends when both parties engage innocently.

What becomes problematic is when insults masked as jokes are thrown out. Sometimes it is difficult to decipher the difference between friendly shade and underhanded comments with harsh undertones. I have never understood the latter, nor have I understood the need to have fun at the expense of someone else feeling bad. I have always thought to myself that there is no point in being around someone who simply tolerates me. Unfortunately, a practice that may have begun as innocent fun for laughs has morphed into a culture led by mean girls.

Maybe you watched the hit reality TV series *The Real Housewives of Atlanta.* For years, I was a faithful viewer; I couldn't wait to turn on my television every Sunday evening to see who was going to get dragged and read for pure filth. Besides loving the fashions and lavish lifestyles displayed by these women, I was thoroughly entertained by all the drama. Over the years, I've have noticed a common theme about this show and others like it. It appears that every season or two, a new woman is presented to the friends and hazed by the group. The new girl appears to be on an audition for friendship in some twisted initiation process.

Although the Real Housewives franchise is meant to be entertainment, we can see these same games being played out among everyday women.

I was raised to be an independent thinker; I have never really had a clique. I could argue that friends from my neighborhood were my clique, but they've been more like family, as I've known them for almost 40 years. I never attended my neighborhood schools. I made friends with one or two people in different groups at each school I attended. I always had close friends, however, if someone new came along, we never played games, at least not intentionally.

I find it very difficult to try and convince someone that I belong in a group and allow another female to throw shade my way and treat me as less than. There is not a woman alive who will make me kiss her ring, especially at my age. My belief has always been that if someone feels the need to shade me every time we have an encounter, they don't belong in my world. It's that simple.

Ironically, women who perpetually throw shade cannot take it when karma delivers them something deserved. Many times, these women are all bark and no bite. Unfortunately, until a victim checks them or something worse happens the attacks, at least covertly, won't stop. Still, who wants to become the focus of conversation when they leave a room?

Who wants to associate with a group of women who is merely tolerating them? Make no mistake: when a woman goes out of her way to continually throw shade at you, she does not care about you and is not your friend.

Shade throwing is often a result of someone feeling envious. Have you ever heard the line "Umm, must be nice."? A woman gets a new car or house and we say "Umm, must be nice." Flown out and given lavish gifts by a male suitor, "Umm, must be nice." Yes, these things *are* nice, sis: very nice! It's easy to be envious. But try not to be mad. God blesses us when we stop hating. He does not show favoritism. What is for us is for us. What is for another woman is for her.

Sometimes shade throwing can be overt: the perpetrator has no shame and does not try to hide her true feelings. At other times, shade is expressed covertly, thrown by a woman who is passive-aggressive. She makes comments that are meant to be offensive with a smile on her face. I have witnessed this type of interaction in social settings. I do not comprehend the purpose behind humiliating another woman just for a good kee-kee. It is unbecoming, catty, disgusting, and unproductive.

Let's be honest and admit that most women who have a comment for everything and everyone often have no right to pass judgement. For example, have you ever:

- Been in the presence of a woman who spoke negatively about another woman's appearance? (I have, and my first thought was the appearance of the woman speaking, not the target.)
- Heard a woman discuss another woman's weight and thought to yourself that she herself could stand to lose 30-50 pounds?
- Heard someone shade the behavior of a woman's child, although

that woman's own children are bad as hell?

- Witnessed someone speak about another woman's hair as you stared at the speaker's unkept lace front?
- Heard someone gossip about a woman's cheating husband although her own man belongs to the streets?

These women usually suffer from low self-esteem. They speak negatively about others in an effort to deflect negative attention from themselves.

Some people find a way to throw shade even when the target is doing something positive. For example, when I decided to go back to school and get my doctorate, plenty of people cheered me on. However, a few people simply could not fathom why I wanted or needed a fourth degree. Even after I explained that attaining a doctorate was a personal goal, these individuals found something negative to say. The comments were mostly about the years of study and high cost of the program, although neither of those factors affected them. They were not the ones enrolled in school, nor were they paying my tuition.

Personally, I have found that it is often best to be quiet unless your opinion is desired. The old saying holds true: if you have nothing positive to say, it is best to not say anything at all.

People almost never reveal their inner struggles. What if we constantly take jabs at a woman who is being abused at home by her husband? What if the target of our shade is suicidal, and being criticized pushes her over the edge? What if the woman we verbally attack knocks us upside our head? Some people have no middle ground when it comes to addressing disrespect. The woman being targeted could end up physically embarrassing the perpetrator. Think twice before speaking. The bottom line is that kindness never hurts.

The thought that a girl or woman's mere existence can make another girl or woman so bothered vexes me. Furthermore, the perpetrator ends up looking foolish because any grown woman would pay her complete dust. Often, the target is not even thinking about the shade thrower, yet the shade thrower is fixated on the target.

It is so true that the woman who gets money does not understand the woman who hates. The goal digger does not understand the woman who has nothing going on in her world. The woman who makes boss moves does not have time to be messy. Instead, she surrounds herself with other like-minded women. This is one of the many reasons I appreciate my village of women. When I'm with them, I am at complete ease. I never feel like I am the topic of discussion when I leave their presence. They cheered for me after each degree, after each book, and after each business venture. It was easy for them to do this because they each have a business or side hustle themselves. They are not threatened by my accomplishments. We discuss businesses, family, and how to win.

I have witnessed women who publicly claim to be grown up and mature behave like childish schoolgirls. If a woman is truly mature, she does not have to announce it. Her actions speak louder than her words. My mother taught me to recognize a tree by its fruit. You cannot claim to be mature when you are continually in someone else's business. Likewise, you cannot claim to be grown up when you are continually throwing shade at a sister. This type of woman has the mind of a twelve-year-old at best.

Like the other behaviors I've mentioned, shade throwing can also damage people's self-esteem. Although light-hearted shade can be fun and entertaining when both parties are participating, we must be cautious about turning shade into full blown personal attacks. It is best to speak with someone as an adult and to express your concerns rather than use shade throwing as a weapon. Lastly, we should strive to treat all people the way we want to be treated.

Reflection and Discussion Questions

1. Have you been guilty of throwing malicious shade at a woman (or girl)? Describe what you did.

____

____

____

____

____

____

____

____

____

____

____

____

____

____

2. Which of your comments or actions could have been hurtful?

3. Do you believe you are envious of this person?

4. How could you have handled or how can you handle this situation differently?

5. Think of a time when someone threw malicious shade at you. How did it make you feel?

6. How did you respond?

7. In what ways do you believe a shade-throwing culture causes women to become hesitant to form new friendships?

____

____

____

____

____

____

____

____

____

____

____

____

____

Gentle words are a tree of life; a deceitful tongue crushes the spirit.

Proverbs 15:4 NIV

To me, the thing that is worse than death is betrayal. You see, I could conceive death, but I could not conceive betrayal.

~Malcolm X

4

Betrayal

Betrayal comes in many forms. The type that stands out for me is silence. It is very true that sometimes silence is betrayal.

I have been guilty of this type of betrayal. I found out that my friend's boyfriend was cheating on her. I remained silent because I was friends with both of them. I felt that it was better for me to say nothing instead of getting involved in their personal business. When I look back, I wished I would have told her the truth. Although I was friends with both of them, I should have remembered that if the tables had been turned, I would have wanted someone to tell me.

I realize that what you do in the situation I just described can be controversial. Many of you have been in this situation and made the same choice I did. I also realize that some women do not want to know if their man is cheating. In fact, I've heard of friendships being ruined because the woman didn't want to know. When the friend came to her out of concern and revealed the devasting news, rather than being grateful for learning the truth, she turned on the bearer of bad news and pushed her away.

In this particular situation, I'm referring only to close friends, not associates. If you are merely someone's associate, I believe you do not owe her anything. With a close friend, before we do or say anything, we should pray. I believe the only way we should remain silent on this issue is if we undoubtedly hear God instructing us to do so.

If we are ever on the fence about this, we should err on the side of caution. It is better to tell our sister friend the truth than remain silent and have her later find out that we knew. That would be a huge slap in the face. It would not be a good look. It could cause her to question our loyalty and commitment to the friendship.

Some of us choose to remain silent on many issues when we should be vocal. This is not isolated to the situation of knowing about a cheating partner. Some of us have been in a social circle and heard a comment about a friend that we knew was false or undeserved. Rather than speak up, we remained silent. Some of us take the phrase "minding the business that pays you" too far. We need to think about placing ourselves in another person's shoes. What if the tables were turned? Would we want someone to speak up on our behalf?

What I have always found fascinating is the woman who is quick to tell me what all someone else said about me. My father taught me to not always trust the messenger. Any friend who can tell me what was said about me should also be able to tell me what she said to defend my character.

Many of us have also remained silent when we've seen our friends engage in harmful behavior. Some examples: excessive drinking and drug use, partying instead of taking care of children, sleeping with married men, looking like a fool on social media, and scamming. These actions do not deserve applause, but instead of calling them out, some of us serve as hype women and yell "Yass!" in affirmation. None of this is cute.

Some of us sit back in silence as we watch our friend beef with her boyfriend's or husband's side chick. Instead of telling our friend to check her man, we encourage her to fight the mistress. Here's a news flash: you can beat up every woman south of the Mississippi and still be weak. Grown women have the ability to use self-control. They know how to express themselves in a classy yet assertive manner. I admit that sometimes putting hands on someone is necessary and justifiable, especially in self-defense, however, a woman who resorts to fighting another woman over a man is emotionally unstable. Furthermore, her anger is misplaced. Our role as a friend in this situation is not to remain silent. We should attempt to talk sense into our friend so that she avoids getting hurt and avoids possible jail time.

If there's one thing I hate, it's a blabber-mouth. I cannot stand a woman who runs her mouth about everyone's business. I've had associates blab about their close friends. Some of the mess I've heard about were related to these friends' appearance, financial state, relationship struggles, and other issues. To be clear, we all (myself included) need someone to vent to. We need that certain someone we can go to for advice on any topic. What I'm describing is not the same as that. I'm describing women who live for gossip.

I have former associates who have confided in me about personal matters. Our conversations will always be confidential. I believe that anything discussed in a friendship should not be repeated. I will never reveal the secrets of these individuals because a real woman doesn't move like this. Any woman who is willing to betray a former friend has no honor and cannot be trusted.

Another woman I have a hard time trusting is one who sleeps with married men. I understand and respect the sanctity of marriage. Other than my belief in God, the fact that I was once was married plays a huge part in my disposition. I won't entertain a man who has a girlfriend, and a married man is completely off limits.

I have never understood the level of desperation and lack of self-control it must take for a woman to carry on an affair with a man while knowing he's married. The key words here are "knowing he is married." I realize that some women may not care, which is a whole case study in and of itself. For the purpose of this book, I'm focusing on the woman who believes her bed buddy will eventually leave his wife. I'm focusing on the woman who believes anything this man says. I'm focusing on the woman that loves this married man and will do anything to keep him even though he has stood before God and his wife at the altar. I'm focusing on the woman who has to celebrate Valentine's Day with him on February 15 or do a Christmas gift exchange on December 26. I'm focusing on the woman who gets left with a wash rag and cold sheets as the married man returns home to his family.

What has fascinated me over the years about the woman I just described, besides her behavior, is the excuses that are thrown out to justify the behavior. When I hear "She isn't the one married" or "He broke his vows, not her" I cringe. These excuses are an attempt to not hold the woman responsible for her actions. For the sake of argument, let's say this woman ultimately gets the married man to leave his wife. Does she really think he will be faithful? You lose them the way you get them.

Sleeping with a married man is betrayal. By engaging in this behavior, you are betraying another woman. Let's be honest and admit that karma has no expiration date. What you sow you shall reap. No one is safe from universal law. Do you truly think you will be blessed with a wonderful husband after crawling off of a married man? Some of you may be married to a man whom you stole from another woman. How is that working out for you?

The good news is that we can go to our Lord and Savior and ask for forgiveness. It is never too late to repent and turn away from our sins.

Reflection and Discussion Questions

1. Describe a time when you felt betrayed. How did it make you feel, and what was the outcome?

____

____

____

____

____

____

____

____

____

____

____

____

____

____

2. Have you forgiven the person (or peoples) who betrayed you?

3. Was there a time you betrayed a woman friend who had trusted you?

4. Did you ever apologize to her?

5. If not, what's keeping you from making amends?

6. If you did apologize, what was the outcome?

7. What do you imagine keeps us from speaking up when we should?

Even if my father and mother abandon me, the Lord cares for me.

Psalm 27:10

A flower does not think of competing with the flower next to it. It just blooms.

~Zen Shin

5

Unhealthy Competition

As human beings, most of us are innately competitive. It is natural for us to strive to be the best in every area of our lives. On the positive side, competition can be a catalyst for innovation and positive change. For example, Apple consistently releases a new iPhone each year. Each new and improved version contributes to the reason the iPhone was the best-selling smartphone globally in 2020 (Forbes). The executives at Apple realize that their fiercest competitor, Samsung, wants the #1 spot. Apple continues to hire the best and brightest talent to ensure that it remains the top technology company in the world. They continue to improve themselves, and as a result, they always win.

Healthy competition can make us strive for greatness by working harder. It can make us more goal oriented, inspired, and focused.

While healthy competition has many benefits, I would be remiss if I did not also point out the problems with unhealthy or negative competition. Unhealthy competition is trying to win at any cost, even at the expense of others' feelings. It can lead to stress and anxiety. Author Bernard Kelvin Clive said "When men do not know their assignment on earth they kill themselves psychologically and emotionally, wallowing in different careers and meddling in dreams of others. They become restless and engage in unhealthy competition living unfulfilled lives." Unhealthy competition can cause us to believe that we are never good enough and that what we have isn't either. This type of competition will cause us to covet what another person has.

Some will argue that imitation is the highest form of flattery. I disagree.

Have you ever had a friend copy everything you did? I have, and it made me deeply uncomfortable. Once this behavior became apparent to me, I went from revering and admiring this person to distrusting her. I began to question her motives. In the end I felt sorry for her and I wondered if she had a sense of purpose.

I believe that imitation is the highest form of laziness. We must be careful not to confuse inspiration with imitation. It is OK to use others for inspiration. It is not OK to steal someone's ideas and pass them off as our own. It is not OK to try to one up friends by copying their every move.

Some of us are vicious when it comes to competition, particularly in the workplace. We use our mouths as weapons. Through our words, we fire emotional bullets meant to cause irreparable damage. Some of us lead campaigns to ostracize another woman or destroy her reputation because we feel threatened. Sometimes we don't even know the woman about whom we speak negatively, and yet we gossip as if we do. I have never understood the level of basicness it takes to use hate as a bonding tool. Furthermore, we must get to know people ourselves, because they could be haters who are motivated by unhealthy competition.

Unhealthy competition is not exclusive to the workplace. It can rear its ugly head anywhere, including in community organizations, churches, and even our households. The need to compete is the reason some of us are still single. Rather than being half of a partnership, some of us would rather rule as a dictator.

I love the phrase "Life is not a competition," although I think a more realistic version is "Life is not about unhealthy competition." Healthy competition can inspire us to work harder and succeed, while unhealthy competition can take away the joy of living life and minimize joy that comes with our achievements.

Our attitudes determine which type of competition we engage in. It takes a certain level of emotional maturity to focus on healthy competition.

Reflection and Discussion Questions

1. Have you ever engaged in unhealthy competition? What was the situation? How did it work out?

____

____

____

____

____

____

____

____

____

____

____

____

____

____

2. Have you ever been fixated on the idea of winning or being #1?

3. What do you remember about this experience (or these experiences)?

____

____

____

____

____

____

____

____

____

____

____

____

____

____

____

4. Have you moved past the desire to compete in an unhealthy way? What facilitated the shift?

____

____

____

____

____

____

____

____

____

____

____

____

____

____

____

5. Write down some ideas for ways you can move beyond being overly focused on winning.

____

____

____

____

____

____

____

____

____

____

____

____

____

Each one should test their own actions. Then they can take pride in themselves alone, without comparing themselves to someone else.

Galatians 6:4 NIV

"The journey into self-love and self-acceptance must begin with self-examination ... until you take the journey of self-reflection, it is almost impossible to grow or learn in life."

~Iyanla Vanzant

6

Final Thoughts

It is my prayer that this book and these reflections help you to examine your hearts, if that is what you need to do. Self-reflection is crucial for personal growth and maturity. The purpose of self-reflection is not to beat ourselves up for bad behavior but to figure out where we'd rather be and determine areas in which we can improve.

Having read this book and answered the questions, what have you learned about yourself or your relationships with other women? What will you work to change as you navigate your current relationships? Is there anything you wish you'd known as a younger woman or girl that may have prevented some of the pitfalls you've encountered? Do you have ideas about how the older generations of women can empower younger generations to love and support one another in true sisterhood?

Examine yourselves to see whether you are in the faith; test yourselves. Do you not realize that Christ Jesus is in you – unless, of course, you fail the test? *2 Corinthians 13:5 NIV*

About the Author

Dr. Jeannita Bussle has been a public-school educator for over fifteen years. Her expertise includes STEM education, socio-emotional learning, and college and career readiness. Dr. Bussle's passion is to give others hope and empowerment by sharing her testimony. She believes that one reason God allows us to experience obstacles is so we may help others make it through.

Her education includes a Doctor of Education in Educational Leadership K-12 and a Master of Education in School Counseling from Dallas Baptist University. She also earned a Master of Arts in Teaching Secondary Education from the University of Michigan-Dearborn, and a Bachelor of Science in Computer Science from Tennessee State University.

Dr. Bussle is the proud mom of two amazing children. Being a mother is her first priority and greatest accomplishment.

For more information, please visit Dr. Jeannita Bussle's website:

www.drjbussle.com

Made in the USA
Middletown, DE
07 November 2021

51447924R00073